The Spiritual Wilderness

The Wilderness Romance, Part 3

Freshwater

Freshwater Press, USA

All Scripture references taken from the KJV of the Holy Bible, unless otherwise indicated.

freshwaterpress9@gmail.com

https://marlenemilestheauthor.com/

Follow this author on Twitter and Instagram

The Spiritual Wilderness: *The Wilderness Romance Book 3*

Paperback Version

ISBN# 978-1-893555-95-2

Copyright 2001 and 2022 by Dr. Marlene Miles

Freshwater Press

United States of America

Contents

Foreword ... 4

Part III- The Spiritual Wilderness

Everything Was So Nice, *Until the Ceremony* ... *6*

Flight Power ... 13

The Spiritual Background Check ... 34

Spiritual Baggage *(His & Hers)* ... *49*

Who Are You? ... *62*

Who Did I Just Marry? 68

Baggage Check ... 75

The Wilderness of Disagreement ...79

Wilderness Demons ... *94*

The Wilderness Cover-Up ...98

Breaking Camp *(How to Break Up with a Wilderness Man)* *107*

Epilogue ... 117

Books by this author ...120

Foreword

This book is about the Wilderness Romances and Marriages in which people have found themselves. We discuss how they got there in attempt to keep others from getting into the same predicaments.

We must take what we learn, even in church, and apply it to real life situations. It is also our job to take what we see in people, from a worldly sense and learn from it by applying Biblical Truth.

If it feels that I'm weaving you into the spirit and then into the world and back out, I am. I'm not making plaid, I'm framing reality. The Spiritual Wilderness about the realities of our Monday through Saturday.

Come, travel this book. Learn and glean. Laugh when you feel like it, cry if you want to, and shout when it's done. And remember, God always provides a way of escape, even from the Wilderness.

Part III

The Spiritual Wilderness

The spirit of man is the candle of the LORD.

But when the candle is not bright enough

To light the way...

Lord be the Light in the darkness

Light my path.

Order my steps, Oh Lord.

Everything Was So Nice
Until the Ceremony

How is it that things seem so great between two people before they get married? Even when living together, in sin, there seems a honeymoon essence to the relationship. But as soon as the two get married, things start to get bumpy. One will invariably accuse the other changing. What in the world happens?

It's spiritual.

From your inception, you have been assigned a *familiar spirit*, one that is to go where you go to see and report what you do, and to find out everything about you. Additionally, you are influenced by the spiritual makeup of the home you grew up in and by those with whom you associate, and generationally by those whom you are related to by blood and marriage. So, this spiritual thing that happens in dating relationships and marriages is related to your spiritual environment and make up.

Attraction

They say attraction is a mystery. The natural mind has ever been perplexed by this couple or that couple, or why those two are together, but not those two. I propose that attraction is *spiritual*. You may say it's physical because men are looking at women are looking to see if they are curvy, slim, voluptuous, or whatever. Women do it too. But what is *seen* is subject to the *perception* of who is seeing it. Beauty is in the eyes of the beholder, so a man could look on a woman with this physical attribute, or that physical attribute and not be attracted to her in a romantic way. But he may look on another woman, with the same or very similar attributes and be attracted to *her*. So even though it's physical, it's *spiritual*.

Emotional Attraction

Sometimes attraction is soulish or emotional. If a person is flesh-led instead of Spirit-led, it can also be reasoned out that they can easily be soul-led versus Spirit-led. Folk who date folk who remind them of folk they know and have previously dated are usually soul tied.

People found it humorous when Ellen, who had complained about her ex-husband, incessantly started dating a fellow who looked just like him. It's not funny; Ellen is soul-tied. She's making soul-led decisions by walking after her emotions. The Bible tells us to walk after the Spirit. But that's not always easy, because emotions can wield a heavy influence since they want to lead. Soul-led means led by the emotions or feelings. Some people are soul-led by logic or intellect they figure out that this is the person they want to marry. Most of the people in that group are in the *what's in it for me crowd.* Although they should be Spirit-led, by the Holy Spirit of God.

Spiritual Attraction

You've heard people say, regarding a paramour or you may have said it yourself, *There's just something about him or her that I just can't describe. I just can't put my finger on it.* You can't and you won't because it's intangible, it's invisible and its *unseen*. It's spiritual. The spiritual things about the person that you are attracted to must be spiritually discerned.

Yes, you have discernment, even if you're not saved, you have discernment. But if you don't know that you have it, you will chalk that *knowing* as a feeling, just a thought, or a fleeting impression. If you don't acknowledge God, He will not be able to direct you and give you clarity on what just *impressed* you. You will think that since your flesh feels tingly, your heart skipped a beat, or you sensed butterflies in your stomach that means that you really like or are attracted to that person. But your tingling flesh may mean your flesh is creeping, and the person who's causing it is a creep. When your heart skipped a beat, it may not have been a good sign at all. It may be something you need to have checked. And those butterflies may have been nausea, your stomach trying to tell you something. After you make a few mistakes, you may be able to look back and say, *I should have gone with my first mind*. Or--, *something* told me. That's something was not a thing at all, but a He--, the Holy Spirit of God. And after you live a little while, you'll learn to read these *impressions* that you get and allow them to work for you.

Why is it so important that we know that we have *spirits*, some good and some bad? Why must we know what *spirits* people have, or are influenced by or have had struggles with, in their lives?

So, we can know how to pray, intercede and how to carry on spiritual warfare. Understandable for people that we're related to or involved with, but what about strangers? Do we need to know the spiritual makeup of strangers? Yes, if they ask you to pray for them, yes. If you're going to do anything with or for them, the Bible says we are to know them by the *Spirit*. But mostly I'm speaking about people with whom we have relationship, and those that we associate with regularly say at work and in close interpersonal relationships.

All of us look for people with whom we have things in common for friendship and relationship. We generally have things in common with people who have similar interests and a similar spiritual makeup as we do. On a deeper level, we have things in common with people who have been through similar experiences or grew up the same way as we did. Many people are attracted to those who grew up in their neighborhood, community, or church or in a similar neighborhood, community, or church. We automatically pick people with whom we have things in common, because we don't want to be rejected, especially in romantic relationships.

A woman with a *spirit of hospitality*, for example, may be attracted to a man with the same spirit, although the natural it is not seen as the *spirit* of anything. They just know that they are very social and have similar interests. They both love to have dinner parties and invite people over.

For example, if you are a drinker, you may want to be in a relationship with another drinker. When you turn on your drinker radar, you may be able to spot another drinker a mile off. Not in a bar, necessarily, or you may go to a bar expressly to meet one. After all, that's what you're interested in, so you hook up with a person who is the same or similar vices, habits, hobbies, and *spirits* as you. Now you're matched with a person who is influenced or possessed by the same *spirit* or same *family of spirits* that you are friendly with or hospitable to… even if they are not good *spirits*…

Your new mate probably has the *spirit of alcoholism,* just as you do. You both have it, but it is unseen. It is usually not talked about; it just *is*.

Flight Power

As the Word promises, one can put 1000 to flight and two can put 10,000 to flight. A thousand what? Ten thousand what?

Angels. One can put a thousand angels to flight and two 10,000. Then spiritually, each person has a flight power of 1000, but together when they are married and in agreement, they have the power of 10,000. To the negative, this is not just a principle for good angels, it is a spiritual law and working on both ends *for*, or *against* you. Careful.

For the average human, the purpose of drinking is for distraction and enjoyment. But to entities (*spirits*) on assignment, it is not just to drink but to cause extreme distraction, inebriation, and disaster, if possible. As long as two people are dating, she has her *spirit of alcoholism*, which is a power of 1000, and he has his, which also has a power of 1000. They each believe they've learned how to cope with and handle each their own 1000. It doesn't mean to have control or authority over the other thousand, but instead to maneuver around it, or even get along with it, or at least avoid conflict with it as if they are walking in agreement. Even if it's agreeing on something negative or evil.

You may ask, what does all this Angel talk, and flight power have to do with me? Everything.

Those *familiar* and other *spirits* that hang out with you are also attractive to and attracting *like spirits*. When you meet a potential mate, you are not just attracted by looks, a lovely smile or beautiful eyes. If you're soul-led, there's something emotional about why you like him. He makes you *feel* a certain way that you like. It's a feeling of a memory that you've probably experienced before, and you like it. It could be his cologne skin, eyes, or hair that makes you feel comfortable with him. But there's a deeper attraction, still—one on a spiritual level. It is so deep that most are not even aware of it. That's why people who have never met in person, can communicate by mail or phone--, nowadays via e-mail and social media, two people could carry on a relationship and could already be *in love* before ever seeing each other, or ever having heard that other's voice.

I know a control freak, who chooses his dates by how weak, cooperative, and desperate they are. It doesn't matter what they look like. This man does admire the beautiful ladies, but he just doesn't want one, because the beautiful ladies are self-assured, and confident--what some men call high maintenance.

I have found that high maintenance to the average man, Wilderness or Semi-Wilderness means he has to:

1. *Actually*, listen to what you're saying.

2. *Actually*, respond to what you're actually saying.

3. *Actually*, remember what you say to him as you continue living and breathing as your relationship is progressive.

4. *Actually*, remember the stuff he says to you, which usually means he can't make up a lot of stuff and you'll just believe it.

5. *Actually*, be accountable for his words and actions in your relationship.

6. *Actually*, help you with your needs and personal issues, which is what you expected when you pair it up with them anyway.

Wilderness men hate the above 6 things, they ***actually*** do.

This particular Wilderness Man himself is more handsome than 10 Billy Dee's, but he looks for and dates the most unattractive, low self-esteem having women you will ever meet. They start out with low self-esteem, and he does nothing to build them up. He may do things to keep their self-image low and even work to make it lower than it is. He is not choosing his dates by the physical, but instead by the *spirit (the lesser spirits, not the Spirit of God)*. When he discerns low self-esteem in a woman that draws him. The women, besides being attracted to his good looks, respond to him because he also has very low self-esteem, even though it's masked by bravado. The *low self-esteem spirits* attract each other. It's spiritual.

Aside from manipulation and the desire to control another, what you **are** and what you have *in* you spiritually draws what you *are* more than what you **want**.

For example, a person who focuses on or watches pornography will pick up a *spirit of lust,* which is governed by the *spirit of whoredoms.* They may be sneaking this demon in with videos or magazines that they are hiding them from their spouse. They may be saturated with it and the spouse may not even know it. Or maybe she does. A good rule of thumb is if you are doing something or want to do something that you don't want your spouse to know about, that's a sign you shouldn't do it, and shouldn't *want* to do it.

Mr. Porn is a type of Wilderness Man who is smitten, influenced or even possessed by the *spirit of lust*. When someone of the gender that he's attracted to comes along, there's a demonic attraction, a demonic charge; it could just be on his part or there could be a charge between them. The devil does have human agents in the Earth. The more in bondage either is in, the more attraction, pull, power or influence the demons have. This man decides that his own wife is not "hot" or "sexy" and may begin to complain.

He's complaining because he's hooked on a demon, and that demon is not *in* his Godly wife.

The more time one has spent participating in or viewing this smut, which he has defined or defended as *harmless*, the stronger the demonic hold. The voyeur may not even realize that anything has happened to him and may even protest that *nothing* has happened to him--, as do most.

Yet, what is *in* him is attracting more of the same to itself. It may not even be what he wants. This pornography thing could have started out as a curiosity. It evolved into entertainment, then fun, then distraction. But now it's taken a life of its own. He may have a beautiful wife and family who may begin to find him weird or hard to be around. Instead of drawing his family, he is attracting what is *in* him, more than what he outwardly **wants, *says* he wants or is expected to want to fit in or look normal**. The more he saturates himself in porn, the more illicit opportunities the devil will send his way, and the more repulsive he will become to his family.

The devil can be subtle. He doesn't always do and can't always do what he really wants to do to you the first opportunity you give him place in your life or mind. The devil sometimes pretends to be a gentleman. He takes his calculated time. It may not make you go all the way on your very first sin date with him. As a matter of fact, you leave those first few devil dates feeling good, thrilled, excited, invigorated. That's the bait. Sometimes you think, *I got this. This is great. I can keep this under wraps. I've got this under control.* You must be in control. You think this feels so good; and it's a secret.

Too many saved and unsaved *think* they are immune to the devil. True, God is forgiving and gives Grace so that even if you stepped mistakenly, or out of curiosity over into sin, the devil may not be able to do anything to you right away. Maybe the devil has to wait until you do it again and again until that sin builds up inside of you before he can take the action that is designed to take you down or take you out. Saved folks do have the Word of God in them, to fight the devil and help you resist the devil, not to become *immune* to the devil so that you can taste what's in God's hand, and what's in the devil's hand and then pick which one you like better, depending on what day of the week, or who's watching you at the time.

People always say the Greater One is in you. The Greater One should be the Holy Spirit of God, but truthfully, it is the one that you've allowed in you. It **becomes greater because it's _in_ you**. As you give it breath, life, time, and attention; it grows.

How can I say sexual attraction is demonic? It's not, if it's between you and your spouse to whom you're married, it's beautiful and ordained by God. But if intimate attraction is between married folk who are _not_ married to each other, it's not of God. When it's between unmarried folk, the Bible says it is better to marry than to burn. _My_ excitement, flirty smiles so much concern about clothes, hair, makeup, perfume is for _my_ husband. His response to the same is for me. I don't want your husband's glances and romantic attention, and he should not think that I had him in mind when I chose anything I'm wearing or not wearing. If so, that's emotional, adultery. That's lusting in the heart, and that _is_ sin itself. It is the precursor to the transgression, which is the physical act of sinning.

The *spirit of lust* is one of the *spirits* assigned to break up marriages. How many ex-wives have you heard of having said to their ex-husbands, "*You could have picked somebody good looking,* or *How embarrassing,* or *What were you thinking?*"

Nobody was *thinking*. Nobody was really *looking*.

Have you ever wondered why prostitutes can be so unpretty but still make plenty of money? Nobody's really looking. It's not about appearance. Demons are driving those people, and in a sense, demons are driving those cars. Demons are stopping those cars on so many street corners. Ask the average *John* what he was doing driving around a certain Red-Light District, and he may respond that he *doesn't know*. Truthfully, he may not know. But that doesn't make it right.

Do you see how people can be so used, and on remote control by the devil?

Do you know how to pray? Pray, don't judge. Just pray.

You may have even heard remorseful men who have destroyed their marriages and families say, *I don't know what I was thinking*. **Nobody was thinking** it was the *spirit of lust* drawing and she had that demon, too. Those spirits attracted each other demonically, and with power.

Why do I say *with power*? Satan is the Prince of the power of the air. Sometimes the illicit tension between two people can be so thick in the air that you can cut it with a knife. *Familiar spirits* are running back and forth, carrying messages from his demons to her demons. Furtive gazes, stolen glances, and sneaky smiles are many times the answers that they that the *familiar spirits* have delivered their messages. Folk can't sit still in the same room with each other gotta wiggle, squirm, walk, move around. I've seen it many, many times. The clothes are often the first give away. The woman is usually wearing something that is showing, or about to show something that she wants to give away.

For thou hast trusted in thy wickedness. Thou hast said, none seeth me. Isaiah 47:10 a

While this is happening, the demons don't realize that other people are picking up on it by the Spirit. Their distraction is distracting. The demons are carrying out their assignments, and the people who are under this spell are deceived. Unless someone helps them by immediate intercession, prayer and intervention, with love, relationships could be damaged or destroyed. If not checked. Many of these deceived people begin to believe that they're *in love*, not discerning the difference between love and lust.

The woman usually believes that if he's interested in her body, she can win him. While the man believes if she's offering her body she wants or loves him. They're both demonically deceived. It's the *spirit of lust* working between them like a child working both parents, as they both have allowed, invited, embraced, empowered, or are just "parenting" their demons. The *spirit of lust* goes to one and says, *"I will if you will."*

When in reality, he or she never consented. *His spirit of lust* consented to *her spirit of lust*. Instead of behaving as mature adults, they let their *children* decide what they should do.

Pray. Don't condemn. Just pray, in the Spirit, and in love. The goal is as an evangelism to deliver the prostitute from that demon. A prostitute is anyone who's offering their body in exchange for something they want, or believe they want. A prostitute can be male or female, and they don't have to walk the street. Neither is the exchange always for money. Often, it's for prestige, position, or perceived prestige--even in the church.

Deliverance is the goal for that susceptible, saved person who is influenced, attracted to, saturated with or possessed by the *spirit of lust* and *whoredoms*, instead of being repulsed by it. I didn't say repulsed by the *person* I said, repulsed by the *presence of the demon*. Don't condemn people who fall for these tricks. No pun intended. But it is his fault that he is not repulsed by the demon. He has viewed it, saturated his eyes and mind with the images of it. He has even sought after it. The devil has convinced him that it's harmless entertainment, by telling him, *It's what real men do.* So instead of being repulsed by it, cringing, or becoming spiritually alarmed, moving into warfare, he welcomes it.

Don't look at me as if I invented adultery, alcoholism or any sin just because I talk about it. If I had, why would I be telling you how to spiritually recognize it and tear down, so your marital relationship will be strong?

As warned in the beginning, don't accuse that the language in this book is too strong. I told you it would be real because this is **real life**.

How do I know all of this? God showed me, and I've seen it many times. I've turned around in church just in time to see the woman in the short, seductive outfit come through the church doors, late--, escorted by her husband or some man. They walk to the very front row. Wow! Walking, talking Wilderness, sitting right on the front row. And I usually never look back to see who's coming into the church after it has started. But it was as though the Holy Spirit said, *"Look,"* and so I did.

I'd seen her assignment from the very minute of laying eyes on her. In a matter of weeks the pastor of the church, that church, that whole congregation, and that man's marriage was in destruction and headed for Hell, while still here on Earth.

Why didn't I do something about it when I first saw it?

At that time, I was single, young, and too ignorant to pray. I thought that some *holy folk*, the ones with titles, sitting on the front rows, were praying. I had no idea that I was the only one seeing this horrible thing; it seemed so obvious. I thought the man of God was seeing through the Devil's plot and it would be a laugh that he'd share with his wife that evening after church as they dined.

I never questioned for a moment that I didn't see it because I know with certainty and by the manifestation of the disaster that I did see it. I will never doubt that God is showing me, and neither should you. God is giving me strong discernment, and for that I praise Him.

The difference is now I know how to pray. Do you?

Woman, if you've tried to, broken up, interfered with, interrupted, or tried to get into any person's marriage by romantic or sexual overtures, you are operating under demonic influence.

Demonic influences also alive when a man creates and tries to create excuses in his relationship with his spouse, with ulterior motives. What do I mean when a husband who is *not* arguing with his wife moves to the guest room to sleep there? So if or when he has the opportunity to share the sorrows and woes of his marriage with a susceptible, gullible, stupid, demonized woman he can quote "honestly" say, *"We don't even sleep together.*"That's demonic, you know. **It's a lie.** Because the implication is that they were *not* having sex. But he's not saying that. He is only saying, *We don't sleep together.* The inference is to be made that they are arguing or not having a real marital relationship, but they are **not** arguing, and their marriage may be fine. But he didn't say that. This is how too many young girls are duped out of their virginity. This is how their opportunity to be with the young man that God has for them is **stolen**. A greedy, selfish, lusting, married, old, Wilderness Man who have already had their own youthful relationships with females their own age and are now lusting to ravage, rape, and destroy another generation. It's barbaric. There's nothing civilized about it.

The sad irony is, after sex with his wife, he may have slept on the sofa because he chose to. The next morning, this man may have *chosen* to shower and dress for the day in another bathroom in the house where his wife is **not**. He may not want to look on her nakedness because he *is* attracted to her. They aren't having a fight. They're not angry with one another. It's something he's *decided* to do so he can play the demonic role that he's allowed the devil to put in his mind. His cry will be, *She won't let me in the bathroom. I can't get in there. She's hogging it.* Or the ever popular, *She won't even undress or shower in front of me.* The implication is that the woman doesn't want him to look on her and she's withholding sex from him. But she's not. And he didn't say that.

This demonized, married Mr. Wilderness is setting up an elaborate scenario. He's actually *living* a lie, so he doesn't have to *speak* a lie when he plays the victim, or the misunderstood, underappreciated, hard-working martyr, which is all still a lie. Wilderness Man, what are you giving your daddy, Satan for Father's Day?

The Wilderness Man will lie, and many times he's an accomplished liar. God is not pleased at his demonic behavior. The wife is not violating the plan of

God in the relationship, so this man will not, without demonic spiritual violence, step outside of his marriage vows or separate what God has put together.

How is he Wilderness?

Remember the Israelites were fornicating and committing adultery while Moses was up on the mountain? How do you think the women were convinced to participate? Lies and deception. Some were willing, I'm sure. But lies and deception are two other keys to the Wilderness. The Israelites used them. Forty years' worth of use, and so does the modern-day Wilderness Man, single or married.

What can separate what God is put together? What fool would try? Not the man, not the woman, under normal circumstances. But the devil will try it. And he tries it through Wilderness People.

God put the sun in the day and the moon at night. Who would try to separate that? The same respect is to be had for marriage. God has put it together, no one shall break it up. No one. Further, if you have no respect for marriage, who will want to marry you? Now or in Eternity? You are expected to be suitable for marriage to the Lamb. Marriage is our ultimate destiny. On Earth with natural spouses, we practice. While single and married, we practice by respecting other people's, marriage or covenants.

Are you running to the devil, telling him that God won't spend any time with you, that God has stopped paying attention to you, or that He doesn't respect you? Are you telling the devil that God doesn't appreciate you and that you don't think that the two of you should be together? If you're telling anything like that about your husband, to *any man who is not your husband*, then it's just as good as telling it to the devil. If that man has the devil in him, you're feeding it, and that devil is growing.

Don't do it; it's Wilderness.

If that man is telling anything like that to any woman who is not his wife is as good as telling it to the devil. It will feed whatever sin is in her that will move her to participate in his sin with him.

Further, the Gospels even say to respect that which is another man's, and God will give you your own. Singles and divorcees, did you hear that?

The Spiritual Background Check

Women have been long teased that they should get a credit, criminal, and/or psychiatric report on their potential mate. What is more important is to get a *spiritual* background check on the person you are marrying, else you may wander in the marital wilderness for a *long* time even after you get married. Not questions such as what denomination are you or what are your spiritual beliefs or church experience? *What spiritual things are in your family history? What choices have you made in your life?* These answers reveal the spiritual makeup of a person. The best person to get that spiritual information from is the individual himself. Don't ask their neighbor. You could gather it yourself and get information by meeting his entire family--, definitely all of his friends and associates. No surprises.

And it is important that you *give* an accurate spiritual background report on yourself, no surprises. Chances are very good that the person won't dump you or leave you or leave you at the altar for telling the truth *before* the wedding. Who could run away from a praise report? Your spiritual history has become an epic of God's goodness, mercy, and defeat over the enemies that have tried to oppress you, hasn't it? Chances are good, since attraction is physical *and* also spiritual, that the person you are attracted to, in love with, and desire to marry has gone through is going through or has a lot of the **same stuff** that's in *your* spiritual background report. So, you two can face it in love, and in the power of prayer and spiritual warfare, or you can uncover the layers of not telling all the truth one day, one week, one fight at a time, and wondered why your relationship is going to heck, ever since the ceremony.

Background Questions

I asked my (then) husband immediately as a marriage talk began.

- What are the spiritual strongholds that you have had to deal with in your life?
- What was the outcome?
- What is the status?
- What familial sins as your family had to overcome?

Then I suggested that we share that information so we could work together to help each other individually and as a couple, to make our marriage a success. Having that information early in the relationship helps you make better decisions. It helps your couple marital prayer life as well. It saves time because you actually know what to pray for. Confession is good for the soul; no one can come along later and blackmail you. It's just you and your spouse without the dramatics of the Jerry Springer Show.

And you will better know how to raise your children and what and how to teach them, or to keep them away from, the based on the spiritual history, of the family.

The Covenant *is* the Promise. God wants to stablish Covenant with us, and marriage is a type of Covenant that we see daily and can understand. When asking these hard questions, even before marriage to my husband, I was looking for the way *into* the marriage Covenant. When kings made Covenant in the Bible, they didn't just brag on all they had and all they could do. They knew each other's weaknesses and needs as well. That's *why* they made Covenant; to cover one another's frailties so that enemies would not take them out at their points of weakness. These questions were not my way of finding a way out of the relationship. I was revealing myself as well to find a way *in*. I was seeking the Covenant, the reward, Unity, and ultimately, I was seeking that God **command the blessing upon us**. And, that God would see each of us as worthy to be married to the Lamb by our marriage to one another.

When you ask the hard questions to even *prove* your spouse, you are getting to know even the shortcomings of your mate and looking into away ***into*** Covenant. You're looking for the way to practice being in Covenant, so when God comes, He can find you approved. By asking the questions that guard your relationship and covenant, you're not looking for a way out you are instead looking for the answers to keep you ***in*** Covenant.

God makes Covenant with us, but He's not acting or pretending that nothing is wrong with mankind. He has full disclosure on how we have all come short. But when he decides to make Covenant anyway. He even sent His Only Begotten Son so that His Blood could stand in the gap for us. That's love. That's not pretending. So, when we are entering into Covenant, should we also not have, and give full disclosure?

I believe that's what 99% of marital fights are about: Disclosure. When you discover something negative about the other person that they should have and could have told you, but they didn't, it cuts into trust and borders on betrayal. It shocks, stuns, disappoints, and causes emotional upheavals. Covenant means tell me about you, and I'll tell you about me. That's what dating is about--, getting to know one another mutually and **willingly**. Discernment only needs to kick in when somebody is not forthcoming. Nobody is ever upset after finding out something positive about their mate.

May I save my discernment for spiritual warfare, or do I have to put on the whole armor of God to go on a *date*? Must I use discernment, the gifts and Fruit of the Spirit and go into spiritual warfare while I'm *on* a date? If it was a Wilderness Date so, probably, yes. No wonder the date only lasted an hour, and I'm so tired! Can I use my spiritual warfare for spiritual battles against the enemies of God, or do I need to use it to sit at the dinner table with my spouse? Hopefully the former.

In making Covenant, face it, you are not perfect, and you are not marrying a perfect person. If you can't accept that you're not ready to be married. If you cannot allow the other person to help you with your *stuff*, be it spiritual, physical, or financial, why are you marrying them? The person who may marry you is the one you choose to help you work out your *stuff*, and vice versa. If the person to whom you make deep confessions can't handle it, throws it back in your face later, then you know they are not mature enough to be married either at this time, or at all. Better to know that now than to do a 40 plus stent of Wilderness years.

<u>You</u> have to make that confession not just things that you've done, but also of things that you've been *tempted* to do, influenced to do, as well as things that you have traveled down your family line. Even if you didn't do them yourself, if your mom, daddy, brother, or sister did them, or we're tempted to do them, those

are *familial spirits* working against you, too. If your aunt or uncle are influenced by them, that will affect you to a lesser degree than if your mom, dad, brother or sister are tempted by them--, but still. People, the only way we will be able to fight the good fight is to expose the enemy.

Ed has the most vain uncle in the world. Uncle Theo is not gay, but he is gray and obsessed with his looks. He is 70 years old and dyes his hair jet black. He keeps his manicure, although he works in construction. Face it, he's a peacock. He douses on so much cologne that if he smoked, there's fear a lit match would cause him to combust. Ed has always made fun of him. But now that Ed is 50, just like his uncle, he has found jet black, *Miss* Clairol, just like his uncle. Ed has given into his same *spirit of vanity*. That's no big deal, you say. Yes, it is. One spirit invites another, and they work in tandem. Pairs, groups and packs. *Vanity* invites *lust*.

Ed's wife is irritated with his peacock-like behavior. Ed doesn't know why saying, *"It's harmless."*

Ed's wife knows Uncle Theo very well and like all of us, she has at least some discernment. It's harmless. *Is it?* Ask me about Ed's uncle. Go ahead, he's married, but...

You may wonder why I keep harping on this. I know about *vanity* and *lust* because it happened to me after divorcing. I was affirming myself in the hair salon, the gym, the spa and then back to the gym. I think I may have overdone the self-esteem thing because one day I realized that I had turned the rearview mirror of my car to myself so I could admire my own image **_while_** I was driving. That was something that I had never done and had never even thought of doing. At that very moment the Spirit of God confirmed to me that I had a problem.

After suddenly being single, all kinds of men were showing interest in me. I was never the kind of person to try to get attention from a bunch of guys, especially married men. When they paid attention to me, I rationalized that *they* just had a problem. I knew from experience that these same men who were admiring me were admiring a lot of other ladies out there, in the church, and in other places. Although I didn't see them do it, I realized that I do not have a commodity on looks or whatever men look at. If I did, I'd have a serious problem. That problem would either be my ego or trying to please a billion men in the universe, or a billion women would want to beat me up, and God wouldn't do that to me.

After I got through wondering what these men's individual and collective problems were, the Spirit of God got through to me that *I* had a problem, else I wouldn't be attracting this kind of attention. **My problem was attractive to their problem.** The *spirit of lust* that came in with the *spirit of vanity* which I had invited unwittingly, was drawing those who were susceptible it. I had no plan to get attention from any of them, but I had let *vanity* in, and *vanity* lets *lust* in. The attention from these men was because I was attracting **what was _in_ me**.

You and I both attract what *we are* instead of what we *think* we are, or want to be, or what we <u>want</u>. What my grotesque, perverted, creepy little admirers were doing in their private time was now coming to light. Their actions toward me were very telling because I wasn't consciously sending out any signals to any of them. I knew for sure that I was not. I had checked myself on that. Looking back, I can tell you which ones in the church I attended before were operating under the influence of *whoredoms* and *lust*. I can pretty much tell you even without discernment which ones had spent time in pornography. Some may have invited some lesser *spirit* in that had *lust* in--, maybe innocently, ignorantly, like me, the *spirit of vanity*. I don't know how they came to have those demonic influences, but I do know that *spirits* recognize each other.

The spiritual makeup of people that you are drawing to you will always mirror what's actually *in* you. What you draw to you will show you, mirror what you *are*.

I immediately submitted to the Holy Spirit for deliverance and was made free of those spiritual interferences. If you don't like what you're attracting, check yourself, resist the devil and submit to deliverance if necessary.

Background Check

Whatever the confession, there is still a risk in confessing to another human. That's why there must be trust, and that's what love and relationship are all about. If we tell Jesus, He won't tell. But as our Earth marriages are precursors to being married to the Lamb, when it's time to bare it all, come clean, be real, if/when we confess to our husbands, they should treat us as Jesus treats the Church. That we don't or can't confess speaks of spiritual immaturity.

The world teaches not to tell our little secrets, and you can see that it's not working. The world calls it mystique. Who wants to be married to someone they don't really know--someone with mystique? Even if you were married to Superman, which of you do not want to know that he is, indeed Clark Kent?

Mystique is a very thin, sheer veil. Anyone with discernment can see through it anyway. If Jesus rent the veil in the Temple so that you can go to God for yourself, then you can bet a veil of mystery can't stay if Jesus lives in you. With Christ, when the reality of who all of us are, and what we are all doing hits, you can be prepared and not surprised. Your preparation or surprise speaks to the *difference* in your marriage. Is it spiritually based or not? What's the difference between your allegedly Godly marriage and your neighbor's, unsaved marriage?

Anything?

After all this confession and exposure, if he says something like, **Your family** *is the one that has the* *struggle with... or we never had this problem in my family*-- take that as a sign to either wait for more maturity to marry or end the relationship. That is full Wilderness, just waiting to happen.

You're Oppressing Me

Woman of God, that Wilderness Man who is proclaiming that you are oppressing him by holding him to a Godly standard--, he may not know it, but he's not really talking to *you*. He's talking to the demons that have him in a submission hold. A man (mankind) is not designed to submit to Satan's imps and demons. He is created higher than they are. He's created to be in submission to God. The man's cries of oppression are not really towards you, but he is saying that he's hurting, so don't take it personally. Look for spiritual interference, then pray for him. More than likely he is oppressed of the devil. He wants to do what he knows is right, what he knows to do. He is having a hard time doing it. Woman, you are telling him what he already knows. When the demon inside of him speaks, it will say to the Godly challenge, *"You are oppressing me."*

Still, the spiritually oppressed man is in the Wilderness, and he does need deliverance.

Spiritual Baggage

Bob conquered the *spirit of alcoholism* years ago. He has rebuilt his life and is now engaged to marry Lisa. Lisa's family has also had that struggle, but Lisa doesn't struggle with it. She gives into it. She slips a drink now and again since she and Bob both profess Jesus and go to church. That's where they met. Bob doesn't know about Lisa's drinking, and Lisa doesn't know about Bob former alcoholism. They get married and BOOM! They are frustrated at odds, irritable and getting on each other's nerves. What Bob, who has conquered this *spirit of alcoholism*, is now being assaulted by that *spirit* because it came into his house back into his life when his brand-new wife, Lisa.

Something he hates so much is now paired with someone he loves. How can he discern between the two? Will he? Or will he just be frustrated and confused? He may not be tempted to drink; this assault may not be at that level, but something is irritating him, especially when Lisa is around.

Bob is arch enemies with that *spirit*; he knows that *spirit*. It has attempted to destroy his life and he hates it with perfect hate; and it hates him. It also hates Lisa, but she doesn't know that yet. He may not recognize this intrusive impression or this disquieting as the *spirit of alcoholism*, but anyone should be able to recognize an enemy when it's nearby. If Bob had never seen it before, it may have only raised an eyebrow or slight concern, but Bob knows this enemy intimately. Not wanting to admit it's the *spirit of alcoholism* or not having been given a name, Bob just knows there's a problem and begins to wonder if the problem is Lisa.

And she begins to wonder, what's wrong with Bob? He never used to act like this before they were married. Not that she would think anything is wrong with *her*, she's justified and embraced her sin. She's never been really drunk, and Bob has never smelled liquor on a breath--, she hopes. Finally, she begins to wonder if Bob is onto her undercover drinking. Being guilty of drinking on the sly, she begins to behave very defensively. The *spirit of lying* comes in to help her keep her drinking a secret. Without discernment, he may be angry at her and not really know why. When they have conflict, she goes to her stash of Southern Comfort, for comfort, cementing the hold of that *spirit* in her life and their marriage.

His & Hers

All the little agitations that arise while adjusting to a new relationship, especially marriage, are not always about emotional baggage as men accuse women of. It's often *spiritual baggage* that **both** parties have.

The Spiritual Baggage in your home are your own *familiar spirits* and *spirits and demons* you have given place to and befriended. And his. After the honeymoon, Lisa unpacked her demons, just assuredly as she unpacked her clothes. Bob's demons already had set up residence since it was his house.

Mary doesn't exactly trust Fred. It's nothing that Fred did in their dating, or since. Mary is guarded, even watchful. Fred blames Mary, saying it's baggage from a previous relationship, and it is, but it's not just Mary's Baggage. However, Fred says it's something that someone else did to Mary that she can't forget. He accuses Mary of talking it out on him. The spiritual reality is, yes, this thing happened to Mary, five years ago. Yes, it affected her, but she got over it. She had been in a couple of relationships since then, and it had never come up. She had never thought of it again. Until Fred. Five years ago, is when she first learned to recognize this enemy. Recognize what?

Fred, who was married before has struggled with but has not completely conquered an *adulterous spirit*. Before he and Mary were married Fred covered that up with activities and distractions. But now that they're married, they spend a lot more quiet time together. Mary discerned that there is something about Fred, that she doesn't' really like. Not because he personally hurt her, but because she has seen that before. Now she knows the damage it can do. She is not angry with Fred, because she has no proof, other than spiritual impression that this is a problem, or potential problem. Proof, in the natural is the fruit of Fred's actions, based on her own Scriptural and spiritual knowledge and experience. Fred has not and will not admit that he has any kind of struggle; and she will not ask him. How can she?

There is much tension between them that didn't exist before they got married. If she asks him that – whew! The roof could explode!

Now is the time to start pulling down this stronghold, not after it manifests as a disaster God doesn't give glimpses into the future or into potential problems so one can say, *I told you so*. He gives them so you can advance your spiritual army of 1,000 (10,000 if you're in *agreement*,) to give a quick and decisive, early victory. And that's to keep you walking in the green pastures of Psalm 23, for example, instead of coming out into a full-blown spiritual war and natural disaster. That's what spiritual impressions and discernment are for. When you get them, your next thought or feeling should be, **I feel like praying now. I've got to pray!**

Mary loves her husband. She cares for his well-being as well as his very soul. Mary can waste days and hours praying, putting her 1000 to flight on Fred's behalf if he doesn't come clean. Fred can deny Mary's impressions if she ever gets the nerve to ask, and Mary can waste days praying about what's wrong with *herself.*

The Wilderness Man loves to tell the woman, *"It's your imagination."* Or Fred can admit his struggle, and his real need for prayer. They can pray together, putting 10,000 to flight, making much quicker spiritual work of this. Or Mary can continue seeking discernment, and when God more fully reveals this to her, through the Holy Spirit, she can work to tear down the stronghold in her husband's life as long as he doesn't resist what she's praying for, it will be done in time. You can see the time investment that the one who loves the most, and who is the most spiritual must give.

But you can also see how much time can be wasted with lies and partial truths. Lies and partial truths attempt to pave the muddy, murky, emotional roads of the Wilderness, dragging you back there. Keeping you in the Wilderness.

Known Enemies

Usually, relationship agitations come by the presence of a known *spiritual* enemy of one that the *other* has befriended or is befriending. But we all know that's true in the natural too. Wife, when you tell your husband that something or someone is bothering you, you expect him to come to your side, your rescue, or at least agree and pray with you.

Spiritually, this may be the more complicated because *spirits* are invisible, like the wind. They are not seen but the result of their presence is noticeable. When your *spiritual* enemies provoke you, don't you also expect your spouse to be on your side? It'd be nice. So how do you make it known that you need spiritual assistance?

Ask him.

Don't Ask Me Anything

A conflict may arise when one who may be puzzled by a certain situation innocently asks a simple question and the other becomes defensive and offended by the question. The questions are in response to observations of the *fruit* of the other person's actions and words. The one asking the question is usually trying to *disprove* what seems to be obvious, but the one questioned doesn't feel this way. They feel as though they are under attack.

According to the often-quoted women are from Venus, Men are from Mars author, "Men don't like questions." When it comes to women, that's true. But I've never seen a man go off when God asks him anything. Or their boss. Or their momma. A question from a sister or brother doesn't seem to faze a man either. Aunts. Uncles. Cousins. No problem. Even relentless questions from the kids get answered. Men don't like certain kinds of questions from *certain* people. Women don't either.

I'll say to the Mars-Venus man, that whole premise is not Biblically accurate. You cannot have me believe that the person with whom I have become one with will not honor my questions with sincere, honest, and civilized response. No matter what he asks, I will not refuse his queries either. If I don't truthfully answer another living soul, I will answer God and my cherished spouse.

Here's the real problem. (You're welcome):

Demons Hate Questions

Demons are usually trespassing, doing something immoral, destructive or illegal in a person's life. They are sneaky, suspect, and insecure. Ask any child who is someplace they shouldn't be or doing something they shouldn't be doing, and they will become defensive no matter what you ask. That speaks to the childish nature of demons.

Demons hate questions.

Prove Me

God loves questions. In the Old Testament, the Queen of Sheba could come and ask King Solomon *hard questions* to **prove** him. Solomon didn't freak out and go into a rage. Solomon didn't hate questions and he had 700 wives. In the Books of Wisdom in the Bible, which he authored, Solomon would have mentioned how to avoid answering a question if he hated questions. Surely a wife or two asked Solomon something at some time. Wife number one probably had the most questions of all. The questions probably increased as the numbers of *helpmates* grew. Plus, Solomon had 300 concubines. That right there was reason enough for 700 women to have at least one question each of him as a wife. I would have asked Solomon how much more "help" did he think he was gonna need?

Kings and judges, who were mostly men, were asked questions all the time, saying the men don't like questions is unbiblical. God loves questions. We are made after the image and nature of God and our Father, God says, **Prove Me** over and again He invites the hard questions.

Every Bible person who has answered hard questions or got *proved* won rewards, gifts, money, and spoils--. every one of them. When we live above reproach in Christ, we should have no problems with questions.

If a man cannot be asked a question, how will he evangelize the world? If there are no questions for men, Jesus would have had to fight with Nick at Night... I mean, Nicodemus when he came to Him at night. The rich young ruler would never have gotten an answer to his question. The sons of Zebedee would have been ignored.

When Jesus asked the man who had been lame for a very long time, **Will you be made whole?**

The man would have responded, "*Are you talking to me?* "The man would have continued his soliloquy, "*What do you mean, whole? Are you implying that I'm not whole? Are you implying that there's something wrong with me? Are you talking to me? Who do you think you are?*

In today's society, that would have escalated to physical violence. Too many of today's minds are like illegal weapons, locked and loaded, locked up with ungodly thoughts and mindsets, and loaded, filled with worldly bullets ready to defend their wrong thinking with their very lives.

Who Are You?

Sometimes emotional and physical violence has been set off by a simple question such as, **Who are you?** That's a good question. Who do we think we are when we are asking the people in our lives…questions? Who do we think we are? Who are we indeed, when we want to know, *How are you? Why did you do that? How does that make you feel? Do you have a struggle with that? May I help you with that?*

Who are we?

We are who we are. And we are who the other person believes we are. If they believe that we are the representative of Christ at that moment, the response will be considerably different than if he believes that we are just Bob or Janet. If they believe that we are wife, friend, best friend or mate, their response will be considerably different than if we are nosy, neighbor, curious cousin, nasty naysayers, or gregarious gossiper. If they believe that we truly love them, if anyone can believe that we are someone who understands and is showing sincere *agape* love, the response will be quite different. Husbands and wives, I'm talking to you.

Deep calls to deep. The one that truly recognizes who we are is the one who will receive the gift we have for them at that time. Receive a prophet in the name of a prophet, and you'll receive the prophet's reward. If you speak to the Christ in that person in *agape* love, rather than hollering in the natural at the natural man, you'll get a Christ-like response, or at least a reasonable response, rather than a natural man's reaction. When you were seen as a concerned, someone who has been through this or something similar before, the response to, *Will you be made whole?* Or, *May I assist you?* will be affirmative instead of negative and defensive and no fight, battle or war will ensue.

Don't Prove Me

Our lives work by questions and answers, if not we'd have no need for teachers, although it's one of the fivefold Ministry gifts.

The Centurion's servant would probably have died if the Centurion or Jesus for that matter, had had a problem with *questions*. Lepers and women with issues of blood would have all died unhealed. Lame would have never leaped, and blind would have never seen.

You were one of those blind. Amazing, isn't it, His Grace? Yet Jesus did not have a problem with **your** questions. Lord, *Help me? Forgive me? Save me?*

But demons don't like questions. There's nowhere in the Scripture where the devil says that he wants to or can be *proved*. Demons hate questions. As

Jesus came to the Gadarenes, a type of Wilderness. Legion's (Luke 8:28) first response was, *"Don't torment me."*

Jesus only asked him one question, *"What is thy name?"* In other words, *"Who are you, and what are you doing here?"* Actually, it was two questions, and the demons hated it, considering it torment. Demons, hate questions, it **exposes** them.

If a simple question sets your partner off suspect spiritual interference and plan spiritual offensive actions. Get engaged in spiritual warfare to pull this thing down. Don't suggest deliverance to your mate unless you want civil unrest in your home. A person who needs deliverance doesn't usually know it. If they do, they don't usually admit it. It's not dinner table conversation. Still on your own or with a trusted prayer partner or spiritual prayer warrior, pray for deliverance and work toward it.

If the person asking the question didn't want to *disprove* what they seem to be saying, they wouldn't ask the question at all. They would just reach the obvious conclusion on their own based on what they're seeing, what they've seen, and be quiet about it all.

It is very difficult to live agreeably and peacefully when both parties are not being straightforward with self and one another. It is also very frustrating when one is discerning, and the other is denying. It is worse when both are discerning the other's faults but denying their own. Still, it is spiritual. The person that you've probably united with in marriage has or has had some of the <u>same</u> trials and temptations that you have had, or having, or will have. One of the purposes of your union is to help one another get through it. It is not to frustrate one another and self by denying what is discerned, at least on some level. Even though it's ongoing, one problem shouldn't take forever; as a couple, you two have other things to do.

In the joining of spirits, when people aren't aware, the negative tends to take the lead in too many times, it takes over.

Baggage is not always emotional; many times it's spiritual. Baggage manifests in the emotions and tries to work through the flesh. Just as you have to learn the difference in the handbags and luggage at the mall, not to pay too much, spiritually, you must learn as well. Else, you may pay too much to keep peace in the relationship, or you may lose by getting out of a relationship that you should stay in. It's not just emotional, it's not a knock off, it's spiritual baggage. You must know the difference and you have to know that this life and relationship you're in is the real thing, it's worth your time and prayer investment.

Who says? God says.

Now, do you know how to pray?

Who Did I Just Marry?

Since that partying couple are having so much fun together drinking and carousing, they decide to get married. But *they* didn't just get married, their *spirits **join***. Either because of the covenant they just made with one another, or because of long term association, relationship and especially physical (sex). *These spirits join.* That means there is an escalation in whatever influences them negatively or positively. More than simple math, the things that they agree on, escalate in influence.

The things that don't agree between them began the classic power struggle we see in marriages, until one of them either wins or the other gives in. Most couples will complain about rehearse and retell the negative, rather than the positive. So now we know about their marital problems. When Bob and Lisa unite between them, they have a *spirit of alcoholism* that has now increased in power exponentially to a flight power of 10,000. Newlyweds, that's a serious Frankenstein you just breathed life into. And secondhand breath it was mixed with *your nature*. Mayhem, distraction, civil madness, in your home and disaster may too soon, and too often follow.

Then that blithely innocent question. *What happened? We were so happy before we got married.*

The "institution" of marriage will receive most of, if not all of the blame. When the real problem is they had some negative things that they should have gotten over, individually, **before** they got married. Now that they have made covenant, the irreverent things that they used to celebrate and do together are more powerful than ever. The demons they used to play with, drink with, don't want to play anymore. Now it's as though they want to make war. Why? Because now it's many-- 10,000. They've got numbers, power, influence and now they want to *possess*. It's as though the demons were childlike before marriage, and now they've suddenly grown up overnight, like so many soap opera children. And we know what trouble they can cause.

Have you noticed that something happens to two nice people after they have illicit sex? They become possessive of one another. It's demonic. After sex, play-demons become possess-demons, the principalities and powers over these *spirits* may have escalated their assignment from *play with*, to **destroy**. It has happened a million times in the natural with so many frozen snakes. It's an old devil tactic: bait and switch. Easy, simple, benign, and seemingly fun things can suddenly become destructive and dangerous when the numbers of things that need management, outgrow management.

When the party demons don't obey, when they don't stay in, or come out on an as-needed basis, it can be very inconvenient and embarrassing for the host.

Hey, many people like having one or two pets in the home, for example. These pets can be trained nicely, but when they multiply to 20, 30 or more, the pets will rule that house.

The combining of *spirits* is usually more powerful than the two newlyweds have any idea of what they're dealing with. They also have no real spiritual weapons to fight problems because they, themselves are carnal. They are natural. They just know they're *in love*, so they either succumb to the spiritual influence, divorce, or both.

Couples who are victorious are the ones who consciously joined their spiritual prowess to advantage. Those who disclosed **before** the wedding enter into real covenant. They participate in praise, prayer, and worship together--, and separately. They maintain and grow their *godliness* together. They cooperate, they confess. When something comes up, they confront it and deal with it **together**. They don't sit around devastated or blaming each other. They trust each other and therefore can **repent** together and to one another. They study to show themselves approved. They talk to and teach one another. They may even fast together. They become a powerful force with a flight power of 10K at their command. They are winners. Once you ascend to 10K Flight Power, you will not want to lose it or give it away for foolish sin. Once you get to know God; you won't want to trade Him for anything in this world. Not anything.

Yet you may be in a situation where you are asking, Who did you just marry? A baby innocent sweet, soft-spoken version of who you're looking at?

Why did they change, you may ask?

Because they could.

How did they change?

With your help.

My help, I didn't have anything to do with this, you may exclaim!

Yes, you did. What you're looking at would have been impossible to create without additive and exponential power of *your* Wilderness demons adding to theirs. You attracted to yourself just what you were, at least on some level, then it multiplied, and increased exponentially.

Get out of the Wilderness and get the Wilderness out of you before you marry anybody.

Note: *Familiar spirit* is not the same as the *spirit of whoredoms*, or the *spirit of lust*, etc. You could think of the *familiar spirit* as skin that is assigned to you and is always with you, and then other *spirits* are blackheads, whiteheads eruptions, and blemishes.

They are additional. They come and go depending on your actions and choices you make.

Whereas your skin is not usually something that you think about. It is just acne and blackheads that you don't notice until they get big enough, demanding attention by hurting itching, erupting and bursting. Demonic *spirits* can demand attention to by acting out, itching, or erupting against innocence in a spiritual sense, or causing you to do things that you normally wouldn't do.

Also, I use the *spirit of alcoholism* as an example. Other negative *spirits* act on flesh in the Earth as well, and it's not always just one *spirit* acting at a time they like to work together further, just because a person is influenced by the *spirit of alcoholism* doesn't make them an alcoholic. The definition of an alcoholic is still the same as you know it to be. However, the *spirit of alcoholism* can cause a person to become an alcoholic; it is only a matter of time, so no demonic *spirit* is desirable to have.

Baggage Check

Baggage is soulish or emotional, when we don't want it around because it hurts our feelings, inconveniences us, or makes us feel some way that we don't want to feel. Baggage becomes spiritual when your awareness of the devastation it can cause is awakened, and you know what it can leave in its wake. Me, me, me; that's soulish. But it's spiritual when considering the long term good of all.

Where is the Baggage Check? There are places to put the *baggage* that men incorrectly accuse women of too often of having. Women of God, a man cannot consistently accuse you of having emotional baggage, as though you have no mind, no spirit by which to discern things; that is abusive. It's just as abusive as saying he has no emotions and no soul.

Mindless spiritless, soulless. So when the Emancipation Proclamation was signed, only **men** were set free? No. When the Hebrews crossed the Red Sea out of Egypt, only men came through? No. God made males, but then Adam made Eve, so Eve now *belongs* to him? Again, no.

But the natural man receiveth not the things of the spirit of God, for they are foolishness unto him. Neither can he know them,...they are spiritually discerned, but he that is spiritual judges all things, yet he himself is judged of no man. For who hath known the mind of the Lord? That he may instruct him. But we have the mind of Christ.

(1 Corinthians 2:14-16)

The Bible says I, a woman, am a soul, and spirit, living in a body, and I have the mind of Christ. Everything in me is working or should be working. A seven-year-old child does amazing wrestling moves with plastic action figures and they never get hurt. They also have no minds, no souls and no spirits. They ask no questions and would make good wives. Somehow, I think not.

So having no soul means no opinion and no worthy conversation that would immediately disqualify women from having emotional baggage because the emotions are in the soul. OK, so women have a soul, but with *only* emotions in it. That's not true. They have **will** and intellect. Do women have no spirit but a body for physical things such as sex, cooking, and cleaning? People, wake up! Men, it's not emotional baggage, it's **spiritual baggage**.

Some of it is spiritual garbage. It smells, and it's easy to spot. We can help you with it if you like, or you can yell and haul off in the other direction. Your choice, like Jonah and like us, you will still have to face it someday. Since you're so adept at seeing it, even though you call it by a wrong name, perhaps you can help us with it instead of spouting off demeaning *emotional baggage* comments. Thank you.

Jesus has a place for us all to check our emotional and spiritual baggage, emotional baggage, and spiritual baggage--, a mismatched set. If Jesus had had that it would be sitting at the Cross to this day because that's where He would have left it, the same place He left His clothes--, at the Cross. And that's where you can take all your baggage, spiritual and emotional. Take it to the Cross.

The Wilderness of Disagreement
(Zero Flight Power)

The Wilderness of Disagreement is far more than just intellectual or emotional. Women may demonstrate or act it out in their emotions, but it's more complicated, involved, and important than the effects it has on a person's feelings. The symptoms of disagreement may be acted out by a man physically by shouting, throwing things, the demonic punching of walls and tearing up houses to include throwing appliances out the door and breaking windows.

Here I speak of rage and rage is of the soul when it is fueled by emotion. But, rage is spiritual because there is a *spirit of rage*. Rage manifests through the emotions and works through the flesh. Men cannot accuse women of being overly emotional when they themselves may not only have emotions, but also exhibit rage-driven, compulsive, uncontrolled, flesh-laden action. Women can do the physical part, also.

Disagreement is a Wilderness that can cause overwhelming spiritual devastation. It is the source of **Zero Flight Power** and manifests by the havoc that it cannot defeat. That is the devastation.

How can two walk together except they be agreed? (Amos 3:3). How can two who agree help but walk together? Spiritually, there is work to do in relationships, not just for and in the relationship, but also for God's purposes outside of, and related to the relationship. For example, when a couple joins a church, they have responsibility to that church. That responsibility is not just to do the physical work or physically be there. It is not just pay tithes and give offerings; it is not just financial. It's all of the things, plus. **There is spiritual work to be done, and that**

couple with a power force of 10,000 is expected to do spiritual work, which may include spiritual warfare.

When you marry, the devil certainly steps up his forces and attacks against you. A 100-member church is not under the same demonic principalities, and attack as a church of 4000. But the size of the church is directly commensurate with the prayer life of the members, corporately and individually. Prayer builds churches. The victory and prosperity of any church is also directly related to the prayer life and spiritual warfare happening in, and on behalf of that church.

With that in mind, who do you think will have more spiritual assaults? A single person or a couple? The couple. When a couple enters into marital union, they are saying to God, "*We become one to do the work of ministry in the Earth.*"

Although I've never heard those wedding vows, it doesn't mean that the two of you have the same gifts callings, or abilities; it means that you two unite as *one* to be more powerful and more effective than a Single.

This is the same as church members becoming *one*, where there is Unity, that is where God commands the blessing. You and your spouse are little version of a church. Just as prayer builds churches and brings prosperity, it builds homes as well.

There are many natural perks to being married: companionship, help, family, et cetera. Those are the extras, but we look at them as the object and purpose for marriage, which can be the problem.

Especially if you're a spiritual couple, you will get more spiritual challenges as you become **one**. The challenges are not all related to *your* relationship, home, family, and finances. Many of the things that you're supposed to be praying for, or against, are related to the world *outside* of your home.

Read the rest of this chapter carefully: Spiritual entities that bring the assaults must be taken out by prayer and spiritual warfare, or they can overwhelm a relationship. But those challenges are not merely *because of,* or on behalf of, the relationship. Being consumed with his or her personal problems is the trick of the enemy. If you are kept distracted by your own spiritual *stuff*, you may miss the big picture.

The relationship is like kindergarten, two people got married and are still working on their spiritual ABC's when God is expecting two mature saints who were old enough to be married, to become **one** who are able to make words, sentences, and paragraphs already. Many of these phrases, words and paragraphs should be spoken, declared and decreed during prayer and spiritual warfare, using your 10K Flight Power, in Agreement, to take the enemy out.

If you don't have this in your relationship, don't look to blame, and don't be discouraged. If you and your mate are only coexisting in a Wilderness Relationship, you two probably aren't getting along. So, we know you're not doing anything for your family, home, community, or church—spiritually or otherwise. You can't even agree on how to get along how to treat one another. These spiritual attacks are not one of the partner's faults, *necessarily*, unless the spiritual things it should have been gotten over before, *I do,* were never gotten over.

The Wilderness of Disagreement is why so many marriages are on the rocks or have been taken out through the years. Instead, look to each other and God for help, support, and victory! If it's remedial spiritual work you need, then do it. Whatever you need to do, <u>do it.</u>

Imagine two sets of footprints in the sand walking first alongside each other, then branching off one from another to go their own way. When the steps diverge, things can get in between. Don't believe all wives tales, superstitions, but consider this: Don't split poles. Don't let you and your spouse's footsteps diverge; **walk in agreement**.

The Bible says, *Everywhere your foot shall tread, I will give it to you.* Where you are treading ***together***, God is giving you victory. But where there is Disagreement, the footsteps diverge, then the devil is *giving it to you.* Why is there so much trouble in the Wilderness Marriage? Divergence. Disagreement. Dissention. When his footsteps and her footsteps are not right alongside each other that leaves an opening for something to get in between.

Instead agree.

If you can't agree, what kind of spiritual warfare are you doing? Tell the truth. None. Once married, you'll begin to get assaults and attacks commensurate with a 10,000-flight power that you're supposed to be walking in. It's no different than a sixth grader, getting 6th grade homework assignments; and college coeds get lessons and homework commensurate with their level of education and attainment. You're expected to do spiritual things in your spiritually joined relationship. If you are not maintaining in spiritual matters such as warfare and prayer, no wonder you think being single is easier. It is, but you cannot go back there just because it's easier or seemed easier. You also cannot go back to the 6th grade once you're in college, *except to teach it.*

Before considering marriage, you've got to clean up your individual spiritual mess. If not, it'll soon be a source of distraction in your relationship and may hinder your ability to **agree**. The Holy Spirit is here to help you do just that.

Two are better than one because they have a good reward for their labor. (Ecclesiastes 4:9)

Two have a good reward. What is the reward and what is it for? The reward is for fighting victoriously. The reward in spiritual warfare is spoils. Translated into the natural, spoils are money, goods, houses, cars, and *stuff.*

In marriage, the reward is **Unity**. Where there's unity, there's power. Where there's power, there's victory. Victory means spoils, and spoils mean prosperity. Where there's **Unity**, God **commands the blessings**. Two have a good reward. Rewards are earned. If two do what they're supposed to do in a marriage, there are rewards.

Here's a word for many: a lot of marriages are emotionally, spiritually, and financially *poor* or *bankrupt.* **The two of you who were supposed to be in covenant are not.** Covenant doesn't mean just living in the same house, sharing expenses, and having kids. You two need to be married and working toward **Unity.** Else is just social; your spouse is someone to talk to or hang out with. It's just physical; your spouse is just someone to have sex with. It's financial-- someone to help you with your bills or to buy you things. **Without the spiritual component, what is the difference between your marriage and the unsaved couple's marriage?** You don't drink, smoke or cuss? Is that the only difference?

Marrieds', you must earn that good reward. The good reward is spiritual for doing spiritual work. The spiritual component is what sets Godly marriages apart from the world. That means not only how you respond or react when the plates or cups of life are passed, but also what you choose to take off of them. What do you do when the Cup of Spiritual Warfare is passed? Do you try to pass on it? Jesus didn't.

Jesus was sweating as blood in the Garden of Gethsemane, saying, *"Let this cup pass..."* But then He realized that He had to submit to the **spiritual warfare of the Cross** to defeat Death, to defeat the Devil. We don't have any assignments nearly so difficult, but like Jesus, we can be victorious. With victory come spoils.

What are you doing *spiritually?* Or are you just waiting for the Plate of Grace? That's just what the unsaved are doing. They too are trying to squeeze all the good out of life and God that they can get.

Then, what is the difference between the Wilderness Marriage and your Promised Land Marriage, anything? Yeah, everything should be different about it. Everything.

So you are in a Promised Land Marriage, the **Cup of Spiritual Warfare** came to you, and you (both) picked it up. God is pleased because He wanted and planned that those enemies would be defeated. That's why He *allowed* them to come to **you**. Not to torment, hinder, or confound you, but to make **sure of the defeat**. He sent those enemies to you to create an opportunity for *promotion, prosperity and favor for you and your family,* and your bloodline. You and you, and YOU TWO were sure weapons of destruction against the enemies of God.

A single person will have their spiritual battles oh, you can trust that. But they may not have been able to master that particular enemy with the flight power of only 1000. A lesser immature, disjointed, unspiritual couple who couldn't have handled those enemies, either. You and your 10,000 were *handpicked by God to do this work.* (That is also another whole book).

Ten Thousand Angels

God didn't send Jesus to the Cross to harass Him. It was because God wanted His enemies defeated and Jesus was a sure weapon of destruction against the devil. Christ could have called ten thousand angels. He could have called 6 legions of angels. Married couples can call **ten thousand** Angels, and God expects you to do so. The spiritual enemies that are knocking on the door of your camp will bring you victory and prosperity--if you have **Unity** because you <u>can</u> defeat them. If you don't walk in Unity, you're not joined properly, if you're not *together*, don't blame God; those enemies are there for you to defeat and afterward, enjoy spoils and prosperity.

When you got married, you said you would become *one*, didn't you? Did you? Have you? Don't blame God if you didn't prepare and bond. Take a lesson here.

In Disagreement, a couple will **not** have a flight power of 10,000. The only way they can even have a flight power of 1000 is if one is *not* disagreeing with the other. Because when one is ***disagreeing*** with the other, they cancel each other out and they have a flight power of 0.

Zero.

When this happens, they're bound. They're bound to be frustrated-- exasperated by their personal distractions and subject to be bound by the enemy. He's tied up her 1000 and she's tied up his 1000. When that has happened, the spiritual assaults that present to them can utterly destroy them, wipe them out. That's why the Wilderness of Disagreement is so discouraging, depressing, devastating. To start out with so much and end up with no power and nothing, can be despairing. Ten thousand, minus ten thousand, equals, zero.

Marriage is very serious people, it's personal and it's real, *spiritually* real. It's not just social.

That's why there must be a Head, (leader). Sometimes the head is the tiebreaker, as it were, to keep the family out of Disagreement. The Israelites were on their way to the Promised Land, and they were not considered to be in the *Wilderness* until they "lost" their head. Losing one's head to the natural man means that the leader is out of view. Being natural men, when Moses went up on the mountain, the Israelites began to act as though they had no internal checks, counsel, wisdom, or understanding. They acted as though Moses wasn't coming back, or that he ever existed. They behaved as if they had no leader.

The Wilderness crept in, and the 40-year calendar began.

When the Head of the house is hearing from God for the family, it is his job to maintain the order that has already been established and set by God. The Head of the family settles disputes and disagreements that may arise in family life. It's God's way, but he also ensures that the family is moving in authority and power when they pray, everyone is praying the same thing. One of the most important roles of the Head is to keep **disagreement** away from his family and ensure that they move in power and under authority.

The marital home, the family—they are a little church with God at the head. It is very telling when a little church can't go to a bigger church *together* and submit to the mission of the bigger church. It tells that they don't have it *together* at home.

Wilderness Demons

STD's, Spiritually & Sexually Transferred Demons

S ome sexually transmitted demons are, *whoredoms, worldliness, lust, greed,* and *avarice.* Others are *fornication, adultery,* and *promiscuous spirits,* along with *alcoholism, anger, rage, unforgiveness, and et cetera.* Basically, spirits are transferred by association, relationship, physical touch and marriage, which includes blood. Sex is a common avenue of spiritual transfer.

Don't even talk about Wilderness Relationships, where one or both parties are having sexual relations with *other* people. Your spouse could be bringing anything home to you **sexually** and *spiritually.* No wonder you've seen people who seem to come and go as they say, their personality is one way today and a different way tomorrow. That's not just guilt. That's the transference of *spirits*. The doses and titration, the stronghold and the influence of different demons is different on different days depending on what the individual has been doing, who they've been with and what that person--, those people have been doing, and how long they've been in the company of whomever they've been with.

It's not you. It's not your imagination. **It's your discernment.** Don't be distracted by being accused of being a nag. If God is showing you something about your mate, it's for that reason. Now go pray. Are you ready for spiritual warfare?

Do you care about the person? Do you care about your relationship? Have you made covenant with him with God at the head? Have you joined together as *one* to this individual? Then you are expected to enter into spiritual warfare on his behalf if he is unable, unwilling, or doesn't see that he needs to. If he is willing, able, and sees that he needs to, then you should join him. As his helpmate in spiritual warfare to tear down whatever is trying to tear him, the relationship, home, and family down. It is your reasonable service. It is why you joined with him.

Have you as a couple created and accepted responsibility for the children or the family that you have? Then it's your responsibility to enter *together* into spiritual warfare on their behalf. Are you doing it, or are you so busy nitpicking with one another? Does the devil have you in a tailspin of distraction?

Have you, as a couple joined your local church as members in good standing? Then you are also expected to enter into **corporate spiritual warfare**. You two should have a flight power of 10,000, together. You are very valuable to your local church and the Kingdom of God. Church wise, you help keep distraction and destruction from coming into your sanctuary in the lives of your fellow Members. As for God, you are to be instrumental in putting all of His enemies **under your**

feet, they are to be under the feet of mankind. It's your assignment and your reasonable service.

We must be compelled to pray and in turn, do *spiritual warfare.*

Here's your cup.

No matter what your husband brings home to you in the way of Wilderness or spiritually transferred demons, you have responsibility to pray for and with him. Just as if you have a lapse and bring some crazy moods, attitudes or negative spiritual influence into the house, he's still to be in your corner and praying for you.

Just as no matter what your children track in the house, it's your job in as parents to clean it up. Whatever they track spiritually in the house, it's your job as parents to clean it up. If your husband doesn't have a clue, you have to clean it up by yourself. It will take longer with 1000 flight power, but it can be done.

Are you a grownup? Then go pray.

The Wilderness Cover Up

Wilderness Marriage is tough. But the hell of the Wilderness *Cover-up* is tougher. *The Cover up?* Yeah. The thing you do when *pretending* that your marriage relationship is fine, okay, or normal--, whatever that is. If you're participating in a *cover up*, you are a lie, living a lie, in the Wilderness, which is full of lies. Why is the Wilderness a lie? Because where God is absent, the devil is present, and where the devil is present, he fathers and fosters lies.

Love covers a multitude of sin. You can cover the shortcomings of your mate, but in this context the word, *cover* means to expunge with the Blood of Jesus.

It doesn't mean to merely hide it, pretend it doesn't exist, or play make believe. Plead the Blood over it.

Now, Are You Ready to Pray?

You may be frustrated with thoughts as to why you were positive that God had a mate for you when you were single, and now that you're married, you're wondering if that was God at all. You're wondering what's wrong with your hearing, your spiritual discernment, and your mind for that matter. You know what you asked for and what is now before you *ain't* it.

Jesus, I know, Paul. I know, but you may look at your husband and think or say, *Who are you?* Yeah. Yeah, yeah, he's probably wondering the very same thing about you. Yet, you know, God wouldn't play a mean trick like this on you. Then you begin to wonder *who* or *what* were you listening to in the first place?

The cover up, is "making-like" everything is fine, but it isn't. You want as normal of a marriage as your friends have, whatever that is; so, you pretend. After all, you've got all the parts that should make a marriage successful. Your husband is tall, dark, handsome, and rich. He gave you a really nice diamond for your engagement. And he's bought you a big, fine house. What could be *wrong* with him? You fear it maybe you. *You* fear that you may be the problem, so you don't tell anyone. Not even Jesus.

Maybe you don't want to look at it or acknowledge the glaring flaws in the relationship. So, you don't.

Things are already bad enough, why complain anymore? Who wants to hear it anyway? And it's only going to make him more angry, then you'll have to deal with that. Worry, anxiety and fear keep you quiet. You've got a bad case of the c*over ups.*

Show me a perfect marriage and I'll show you Jesus and the unblemished Church of the End Times (Ephesians 5:27). Of course, Jesus has the discipline, Wisdom, and time to wait for the Church without spot, blemish, or wrinkle. Humans don't, at least they behave as though they don't, and they shouldn't. A blemish free, spot free, and wrinkle free human is an impossibility. One without wrinkles is usually too immature, one without blemishes is not human, and one who's mature will surely have wrinkles. Jesus can ask for and expect the perfect Bride. Who else among us can? Be for real.

Jesus has no biological clock that's ticking like a timebomb waiting to explode about the same time that the Church exhales. Jesus is in His glorified Body. He is Eternal and lives in Eternity. Nothing on Jesus is ticking; He's got time. So where's the perfect Bride? The window when blemishes are gone, maturity is there, but there are no wrinkles may be very narrow. In the natural, what is the perfect age, 33? 35? Who knows? Spiritually, the secret is to arrive at perfection, maturity and maintain it by times of refreshing in the Lord, until He comes for you. But no human is perfect.

Don't wander in the Wilderness of the *cover up;* that's real baggage. Tell somebody; try Jesus. You can't carry all that baggage around. The more you and your spouse aren't moving in Unity, praying together, and entering into warfare and worship together, the more baggage is attaching to your relationship.

You don't have to bring all your dirty laundry to church or the beauty salon, but if you must, then do it. Do it discreetly. Jesus is a great listener. If you ask for wise counsel, and then listen, He'll answer you. He'll advise you well. Just as you have to wash dishes, and dust end tables, you have to purge the baggage ever so often from your relationship, else it just builds up. Even formerly, baggage-free people can get laden down over months and years of misunderstandings, hurts and offenses proving that they are not walking in Unity, and this further keeps them from Unity.

After you've done the human thing and vented, now it's time to re-in-VENT your strategy. Instead of just venting, try intervening; get into your prayer closet and pray. Be bold. Call forth the characteristics you asked God for in a spouse. Call him forth! Call for those characteristics that you know God promised you and that you saw when you first met your mate. Call forth those traits in yourself that may not have surfaced yet, that will, in turn bring out the best in your spouse. God wasn't playing with you; your mate probably *does* have those traits that you desire him to have. Maybe they need to be stirred up, coaxed out, encouraged to rise to the surface. Maybe he needs help, support, and positive reinforcement. If he were already a shiny, perfect diamond when you met him, you may not have met him. Someone else may have picked up that diamond before you--, maybe the someone for whom it was not intended.

The attributes, gifts, skills, and abilities in the package called your spouse may be packaged for your eyes only. If you don't see the best in him, it could be that no one on Earth ever will. (And vice versa.) Be diligent to see if you've overlooked a lot of the good that you're supposed to be seeing.

Surely, you've seen teens where one wears the heart locket, and the other wears the key? Perhaps what's locked up in your spouse, the pastor, or the prophet, that evangelist, and the teacher can't get it unlocked? Perhaps it's only the covenanted marriage partner who can unlock that precious gift. The gift is probably for *you* anyway; you will probably the only one who has the key to unlock that special God-given gift. (Not Gifts of the Spirit.)

The same may be true of your locked away gifts that are for him only. If you receive your husband in the name of the Office of Husband, you will receive the husband's reward.

After you've done all, you know how to do to unlock, stir up, unleash, encourage your mate, you may find yourself in the very same place. If all that work doesn't work, ask yourself:

- Did I have faith enough?
- Is there Agreement in our home?

Yes? Then the next step is to run straight to Jesus to get help. Get Him to help you do what the Holy Spirit leads you to do.

- If it's forgiveness, do it.
- If it's counseling, do it.
- If it's spiritual education, get it.
- If it's prayer and intercession, do it.
- If it's patience and endurance; is this your test or his?
- If it's to develop a Fruit of the Spirit in one or both of you, do it.
- Tithes, offerings worship, fasting-- any of the disciplines; do it.
- If one or both of you needs deliverance, get it.
- If it's all of the above, or any combination, do it.

Stop covering up and get back under *Covering*. Get back in step with Jesus.

The Cover-up Wilderness probably lasts more than 40 years or can seem like it. A façade of a marriage will only interfere with your purpose and destiny for being on Earth. It is a distraction, and it is not of God. That you are emotionally or financially uncomfortable is not the *real* issue. All relationships, especially your marriage should enhance and promote Purpose and Destiny, not hinder it. You, you two, all you do, and your relationship should glorify God.

Come out of the Wilderness and walk in the promise of a good or wonderful marriage. Ask for and get the help you need, whether in the natural or by the Holy Spirit, or both. Shame and blame are not part of the game. If your marriage is lame, don't defame or profane; proclaim and profess and confess. If you want to be blessed, you'll have everything to gain!

Breaking Camp

How to Break Up With a Wilderness Man

Ayoung man once auditioned very well for my attention. I told him that God had put me in his life, as a friend only. I described this friendship, as also having a *season* (a time limit). He was advised that when God told me to *break camp*, I was breaking camp. He didn't believe me.

Instead, he told me that I was just the kind of girl he was looking to marry. Staying away from the evangelistic perversion that I've warned you of, I kept up my witness to him. As time passed, he was responding to me, but not to the Word of God. Gently, I'd urge him to look at God and away from me and reminded him that when God told me to break camp,

I was breaking camp. Still, he didn't believe me. Because he was very attractive in a worldly way and knew it, and because he had financial and other things going for him, he viewed me as a conquest, and with confidence decided he would win. He even told me that no one could *pull* from him.

I told him that God could **pull** from him and when it was time to break camp, I was breaking camp.

God can pull anyone out of a Wilderness of any kind, and He can pull the Wilderness out of the person if they allow Him.

The above example is similar to but different than being married to chronic Wilderness Man, but the question still arises, how do you *break camp?* You just do it. You don't make a long, drawn-out discussion of it. You don't make threats about it for 10 or 12 years. You don't tell everyone you know. You may not tell anyone you know. You have a plan, you have a place to live if you have to move. You have a way to take care of yourself, as you probably always have.

You just do it. Break camp.

I'm not telling you to do anything you wouldn't do already. I'm not telling you to do anything that God has **not** told you to do. I'm *not* telling you anything against the Holy Spirit, but if God has told you to *break camp*, that is how you do it. Just do it. Don't be double minded about it. Don't waiver. Don't vacillate, just do it.

What if he cries? What if he does? What if you do? Haven't you been crying for 40 years already? Are his tears more precious than yours, to God? I don't think so. Saved Woman of God many times the tears are a ploy and mask the need for ***deliverance***.

What if he promises to change? Hasn't he done that before?

Leave him. Then let him change. You may have been the one keeping him from changing anyway. You may have been an enabler to him. A spoiled man most often equals a Wilderness Man.

You leave--then and only **if** you feel like it in six months or a year, call him, if he's not married or in a relationship. Time apart might be good for you, too. Maybe you won't put up with so much junk in your next relationship, or if you two get back together.

In trying to leave the Wilderness, what if the Wilderness Man threatens you? He's done that before, hasn't he? Then you should have been gone. You're afraid. It takes courage. Take some real action. Call proper authorities or agencies to make the move to break from a dangerous Wilderness Romance.

That's Not an Oasis, That's a Kiddie Pool

But of the most importance, get out of the Wilderness! Break up the Wilderness Camp! There you are, in a Wilderness with this man desperately looking for a haven, an Oasis, for love, and other things. Women, wearing too much patience, often wander the Wilderness far too long. Instead of rising from where

110

they were, when they met Mr. Wilderness, they start acting just like that Wilderness Man. They help him forage for food and water and live in survival mode! Then suddenly dry season after dry season, low and behold, an Oasis in the desert. Finally! I've told you that no one ever finds a mirage, without looking for the real thing. So instead of a refreshing pool and a break from the arid humdrum, here's a kiddie pool. It's about 4' X 4' with two feet of water. Worse, what was once blue water is not blue, or clear anymore. Remember, it's a kiddie pool.

Women, in their benevolent generosity, often think that they'll just step into the kiddie pool for a few minutes, then convince him to get out of the kiddie pool and get into the adult arena of life. Guess what, instead of persuading him, it's Scriptural to take on *his* nature, not the other way around. Warning: If you don't like his nature, don't hook up with him. You won't change him, he'll influence you. Then for 10 years, there you are in the Wilderness Kiddie Pool with him, hating every moment, resenting every step and cowering, stooping, trying to stay covered by the dearth of water that's in it. And that's played-in, unclean, played-out water.

The first thing you must do when you break camp is to also **leave** the Wilderness. If you break camp with a gentleman because he's Wilderness and you never leave the Wilderness, you'll just enter into another Wilderness Romance. You could have saved time, money and energy and just stayed with the first Wilderness Man. You must move into soul prosperity and completely and entirely leave the Wilderness for the Promised Land.

Beloved, I wish above all things that thou mayest prosper and be in health, even as my soul prospers.

(3 John 1-2)

In the Promised Land, there will be some non-Wilderness folk who will recognize and welcome you. The one that God *intended* for you, will probably be there wondering what took you so long anyway?

I promise you, if God told you to leave, He's made a way of escape. Slavery and bondage was over years and years ago. God did not intend that His people remain in bondage. Escape! Break camp! Make a run for it. If God said, do it, He would part the Red Sea for you.

The *old man* can't get into the Promised Land--, neither his old man, nor yours. He will have to *change* first Is that what has been keeping you in the Wilderness? Is it spiritual?

It is spiritual if you need to be saved. It's soulish if you are saved, but you don't know how to behave yourself in a saved, and mature way. It's social if you haven't learned to behave yourself, or if you still consistently associate with other Wilderness people. Either way, whether it's spiritual or emotional baggage, check it at the Cross, and come on in. The Promise is the Promised Land!

Therefore, if any man be in Christ, he is a new creature: old things are passed away; behold, all things are become new. (2 Corinthians 5:17)

Epilogue

In your life, do you go <u>around</u> or *through* the Wilderness? It depends on you and God's plans and purposes for you. Some very fine men of God went *through* the Wilderness.

- Joseph and his enslavement.
- Moses and his desert?
- Abraham and his travels.
- David in his cave.
- Elijah in his cave.
- Jonah's storm, whale, gourd, and scorching sun.
- Hosea, and his Wilderness Romance.
- Daniel and his pit.
- Then Joseph had a deeper Wilderness within his enslavement. A Wilderness Enslavement, and a

Wilderness Prison. So there are *levels* of Wilderness.

The Purpose of the Wilderness

The Wilderness is where you learn to:

- Seek God.
- Talk to God.
- Hear God.
- Listen to God.
- Obey God.
- Love God.
- Honor and respect God.
- God only.
- Make Him Lord.
- Make Him love.
- Make Him your life.

You will stay in the Wilderness until you get your romantic ideals together. Romance with God ***first.*** Make Jesus the Love of your life. This is not really exclusion of Earth relationships, marriage and family.

God commands us to be fruitful and multiply, but to seek God and His Kingdom first.

How to Avoid the Wilderness

& the Wilderness Man

Learn what a Promised Land Romance is and set your sights and expectation on having that, so when a Wilderness Temptation comes along, you can resist it.

If you aren't involved in a Godly romance already with God and a Godly mate--, do that. Only Wilderness People will bother you while you're already in a relationship, so that pretty much defines who *they* are.

The above recommendations to skirt around the Wilderness won't always work. Sometimes God will bring the Wilderness to you. Many fine men of the Bible were not considered Wilderness Men but ended up in Wilderness situations.

- John the Divine at Patmos.
- Paul and Silas in prison.

Stay out of sin. Sin, its iniquity, transgressions and punishments are the master of all master keys to the Wilderness. Even if you sneak to sin, it will find you out. The Wilderness will hunt you down and suck you in until you confess and repent of your sin. It's not worth it. It really isn't.

The Wilderness is a risk just for being in the world, even if you're not *of* it. If you're going *through* the Wilderness and it's not to correct your character or get slavery to the world out of you, then it's for another reason. Just as Jesus had to traverse this route to rescue us, perhaps you should be rescuing, not romancing, someone. Have you ever considered that? So, as long as you're in the Wilderness, or going through it, why not bring someone else out with you-- not to marry you, but for marriage to the Lamb?

What man of you having an hundred sheep, if you lose one of them, doth not leave the ninety and nine

in the wilderness and go after that which is lost until
he find it. (Luke 15:4)

Why are **you** in the Wilderness? Why does God *allow* Wilderness? The above Scripture says that if one is lost, He will go leave the majority, the 99 in the Wilderness to go get the one. He does not desire that one would be lost. Not one.

So why is there Wilderness? Why are there Wilderness men, women, children, employers, marriage and situations, etc.

Because there is still at least one lost.

Back in the old days, when you were stringing up your Christmas light strands, if one bulb was missing, broken, or burnt out, the entire strand would not light. We're all very much connected to one another, so why don't you do your part and got get that lost, missing, broken, or burned out *one*.

There's one who's romancing the wrong thing, and they're probably going around and around in the Wilderness. Go ahead, go get that *one*, so we can all step into God's marvelous light and shine, in the eyes of our Father.

Other books by this author, on amazon and/or Kindle:

AK: The Adventures of the Agape Kid

AMONG SOME THIEVES

Churchzilla, *the Wanna-Be, Supposed-to-be Bride of Christ*

Demons Hate Questions

Don't Refuse Me, Lord (4 book series)

Don't Say That to Me

every apple

The Fold (4 book series)

> **The Fold (Book 1)**

> **Name Your Seed (Book 2)**

> **The Poor Attitudes of Money (Book 4)**

> **Do Not Orphan Your Seed**

got HEALING? Verses for Life

got LOVE? Verses for Life

got money?

How to Dental Assist

Let Me Have A Dollar's Worth

Man Safari, *The*

Marriage Ed. *Rules of Engagement & Marriage*

Made Perfect in Love

Power Money: Nine Times the Tithe

The Power of Wealth *(forthcoming)*

Seasons of Grief

Seasons of War *(forthcoming)*

The Spirit of Poverty *(forthcoming)*

Warfare Prayer Against Poverty

When the Devourer is Rebuked

Wilderness Romance, *The* (3-book series)

> ***The Social Wilderness***
>
> ***The Sexual Wilderness***
>
> ***The Spiritual Wilderness***

Journals & Devotionals by this author:

The Cool of the Day – *Journal for times spent with God*

He Hears Us, Prayer Journal *in 4 different colors*

I Have A Star, Dream Journal kids, teen, young adult & up.

I Have A Star, Guided Prayer Journal, *2 styles: Boy or Girl*

J'ai une Etoile, Journal des Reves

Let Her Dream, Dream Journal *in multiple cover colors*

Men Shall Dream, Dream Journal, *(blue or black)*

My Favorite Prayers (multiple covers)

My Sowing Journal (in three different colors)

Tengo una Estrella, Diario de Sueños

Wise Counsel (Journal in 2 styles)

Illustrated children's books by this author:

Be the Lion (3-book series)

Big Dog (8-book series)

Do Not Say That to Me

Every Apple

Fluff the Clouds

I Love You All Over the World

Imma Dance

The Jump Rope

Kiss the Sun

The Masked Man

Not During a Pandemic

Push the Wind

Slide

Tangled Taffy

What If?

Wiggle, Wiggle; Giggle, Giggle

Worry About Yourself

You Did Not Say Goodbye to Me

www.ingramcontent.com/pod-product-compliance
Lightning Source LLC
Chambersburg PA
CBHW060506280326
41933CB00014B/2885